FACT or PHONY?

BLACKBEARD'S HEADLESS BODY SWAM AROUND HIS SHIP!

Aarrgghh!

The Fact or Fiction Behind **PIRATES**

ADAM SUTHERLAND

Gareth Stevens
PUBLISHING

Please visit our website, www.garethstevens.com.
For a free color catalog of all our high-quality books,
call toll free 1-800-542-2595 or fax 1-877-542-2596.

Cataloging-in-Publication Data
Sutherland, Adam.
The fact or fiction behind pirates / by Adam Sutherland.
p. cm. — (Fact or phony?)
Includes index.
ISBN 978-1-4824-4271-7 (library binding)
1. Pirates — Miscellanea — Juvenile literature.
2. Common fallacies — Juvenile literature.
I. Sutherland, Adam. II. Title.
G535.S88 2016
910.4'5—d23

Published in 2016 by
Gareth Stevens Publishing
111 East 14th Street, Suite 349
New York, NY 10003

Copyright © 2016 Wayland / Gareth Stevens

Editor: Debbie Foy
Design: Rocket Design (East Anglia) Ltd
Illustration: Alex Paterson

All illustrations by Shutterstock, except: 4, 17, 20, 28, 41,
47, 54-55, 62, 66-67, 71, 76, 81, 84, 90-91, and 92.

Printed in the United States of America
CPSIA compliance information: Batch CW16GS: For further information contact Gareth Stevens, New York, New York at 1-800-542-2595.

THERE'S A LOT OF NONSENSE
WRITTEN ABOUT PIRATES...

read on!

Read this part first...!

Peg legs, eye patches, parrots, and pieces of eight — that's how we like to think of pirates. Old films like *Treasure Island*, and even the Hollywood hit series *Pirates of the Caribbean*, show a far-from-factual view of the salty old raiders who sailed the ocean blue to find fame and fortune.

If these movies are to be believed, pirates will rob your gold, make you walk the plank, then have a sing-song with a bottle of rum!

But is any of that actually true?

In **Fact or Phony**'s *Blackbeard's Headless Body Swam Around His Ship*, we'll answer all-important questions such as:

1. Did pirates *really* carry parrots on their shoulders?

2. Were pirates always hunting for buried treasure?

3. Did pirates make their victims walk the plank?

You might be surprised to read the answers!

Apart from some head-scratching pirate myths, we've also collected together the best pirate slang, discovered the most gruesome pirate punishments, unearthed some mind-boggling pirate nicknames, and generally put together an awesome book on pirates and pirate history with all the gory bits left in and all the boring bits left out. Just how you like it!

So, here at **Fact or Phony** Headquarters, we advocate that the next time you hear someone spouting an old myth about pirates, put them straight. And then make them walk the plank. (Just kidding!)

read on!

5

So you might hear myths like...

Pirates made maps of buried treasure

Everyone knows that pirates drew treasure maps, right? They robbed unsuspecting ships, sailed to the nearest uninhabited island, buried a big chest full of loot and came back for it later, when the heat was off. Or did they?

★ And the truth is...

Wrong! Pirates rarely buried their treasure. They tended to share it and spend it as quickly as they earned it. No point in burying it, when you might be dead the next week. Better to enjoy it while you could! The only pirate known to have buried treasure was the Scotsman William Kidd (aka Captain Kidd), who is believed to have buried at least some of his ill-gotten gains on Long Island in 1699 before sailing into New York. Like many pirate myths, the idea of buried treasure and treasure maps comes from Robert Louis Stevenson's book *Treasure Island*, first published in 1883.

Verdict:  **PHONY**

Pirates carried parrots on their shoulders

Who can imagine a proper pirate without a parrot perched on his shoulder? Not us!

⭐ And the truth is...

Here's one myth that could well be true. Pirates — and other seafarers to the West Indies and far-flung tropical islands — often brought back colorful feathered friends as souvenirs of their travels. Parrots were more popular than monkeys because they could be taught to speak and to play tricks, which helped pass the time on long journeys, and they didn't poop everywhere. (Not something that could be said for monkeys!) Pretty Polly also fetched a pretty penny when the pirates arrived back in Europe.

Verdict:

Pirates made their victims walk the plank

Not content with robbing the loot from captured ships, pirates are supposed to have enjoyed forcing their captives off a wooden plank into the sea! Couldn't they swim to safety, we hear you ask? Not tied up, blindfolded, and even weighed down with cannonballs, they couldn't! But did this gruesome ritual ever really happen?

And the truth is...

No one knows for sure whether walking the plank is fact or fiction, but we believe there's enough evidence to back up the story. Back in 1769, mutineer George Wood confessed that he and his crew had forced their officers to walk the plank when they took control of their ship. By 1788, the phrase "walking the plank" was even included in the *Dictionary of the Vulgar Tongue* (an old-fashioned equivalent of a book of slang), and in 1829, *The Times* newspaper reported that the crew of captured ship *Redpole* were made to walk the plank by their captors. That's good enough for us!

Verdict: (probably) FACT

"AVAST, LANDLUBBERS!"

A guide to pirate lingo

If you want to talk the talk (but not walk the walk), follow our guide to talking like a pirate and you'll be chattering with your shipmates in no time.

NO 1. AHOY THERE, ME HEARTIES!

"Ahoy" or "ahoy there!" was the pirates' version of "Aloha," simply meaning "Hello." Although it was sometimes also used for "Goodbye" — just to be confusing. "Heart" was a slang term for "stout heart" and so "hearties" were usually friends or sometimes just fellow sailors. The expression gradually changed from "My hearts" to "my hearties" and finally "me hearties" in the 19th century.

THE MOST
TERRIFYING
SHIPS AT SEA

IF YOU WANTED TO STRIKE FEAR INTO THE HEARTS OF YOUR ENEMIES, IT HELPED TO HAVE A SUITABLE NAME FOR YOUR SHIP. HERE ARE OUR FAVORITE SCARY (AND NOT-SO-SCARY) TITLES:

BLACK JOKE
CAPTAINED BY BENITO DE SOTO

SUDDEN DEATH
CAPTAINED BY DERDRAKE

QUEEN ANNE'S REVENGE
CAPTAINED BY BLACKBEARD (EDWARD TEACH)

DELIGHT
CAPTAINED BY FRANCIS SPRIGGS

SEA KING
CAPTAINED BY
BARTHOLOMEW
ROBERTS

REVENGE
CAPTAINED BY
BENITO DE SOTO

FLYING DRAGON
CAPTAINED BY
EDMUND CONDENT

NEW YORK
REVENGE
CAPTAINED BY
WILLIAM KIDD

SPEEDY RETURN
CAPTAINED BY
JOHN BOWEN

TIGER
CAPTAINED BY
SIR RICHARD
GRENVILLE

SNAP DRAGON
CAPTAINED BY
CAPTAIN GOLDSMITH

11

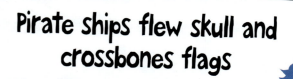

Pirate ships flew skull and crossbones flags

The skull and crossbones flag must be one of the most memorable images of pirates. But did pirate ships actually fly it?

⭐ And the truth is...

Well, yes, they did. The Jolly Roger flag, as it was known, usually consisted of a black background with a human skull above two bones in an X arrangement. But not every pirate ship flew the same flag. Many pirates invented their own flags with crossed cutlasses, skeletons, and even hearts dripping blood. Here are a few of our favorites:

RICHARD WORLEY

Believed to be one of the first pirates to fly the skull and crossbones, Worley's own flag design placed the skull on top of two crossed bones. Worley had a short but successful pirate career — he was captured in Jamestown, Virginia, and hanged in February 1719 along with 19 of his men.

EDWARD ENGLAND

Irish-born England (figure that one out!) invented the skull above crossed bones flag. He sailed the African coast and the Indian Ocean from 1717-20 and was said to be a rather nice chap (for a pirate). He only tortured victims as a last resort.

JOHN RACKHAM

Cuban-English pirate Rackham favored a skull over crossed cutlasses on his flag — a design that was also flown on Jack Sparrow's ship the *Black Pearl* in *Pirates of the Caribbean: The Curse of the Black Pearl*.

BLACKBEARD

Bristol-born Edward Teach boosted the fear factor on his flag with a full skeleton-devil holding an hourglass (meaning "Your time is running out") and stabbing a bleeding heart!

NED LOW

English pirate Low started out using the same flag as Blackbeard, before designing his own in 1723 — a red skeleton on a black background. Apparently Low also flew a green silk flag with a yellow figure blowing a trumpet — this was to call his fleet's captains aboard his ship. It was before mobile phones, of course.

Verdict: (mostly)

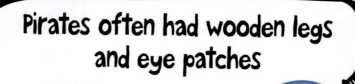

Pirates often had wooden legs and eye patches

Long John Silver wouldn't have been half as scary with two legs, would he? But did real pirates have eye patches and wooden legs, or is that just another made-up Hollywood story?

★ And the truth is...

Well, this one is actually real! Ships' cannons could cause terrible injuries, smashing faces and squashing legs. Surgeons were rare on board ships, but luckily, the ship's carpenter was on hand to saw off damaged limbs before infection set in, and replace them with wooden ones! The most famous "Captain Hook" was Turkish pirate Oruc Reis, who lost his arm in a battle in the Mediterranean and had it replaced with a metal hook for a hand. Always painful when he picked his nose, though.

Verdict:

"AVAST, LANDLUBBERS!"

A guide to pirate lingo

If you want to talk the talk (but not walk the walk), follow our guide to talking like a pirate and you'll be chattering with your shipmates in no time.

NO 2. SHIVER ME TIMBERS

An expression similar to "Ooh, fancy that" or "Blow me down" but of course much scarier! It was used to show a pirate's shock or disbelief, and is believed to have come from the sound a ship made when it ran aground or was hit by a cannon blast and the timbers, or wood, on the ship shook.

> # Blackbeard set fire to his beard before attacks to scare victims

Edward Teach was the Harry Styles of pirates — everyone knew his name! It's believed that Blackbeard was born in Bristol, England in around 1680 (although no one knows for sure), and started life as an honest(ish) sailor on privateer ships, cruising the East Coast of America and the Caribbean. Settling on the island of New Providence in the Bahamas, Blackbeard decided to turn his hand to piracy and joined Benjamin Hornigold's crew. Hornigold quickly gave Blackbeard control of his own ship and together they stole flour, rum, and wine from unfortunate ships that crossed their path.

And the truth is...

Blackbeard was a clever and cunning pirate who mainly used his fearsome image to get what he wanted. Prisoners were so frightened of what he might do that they usually surrendered without a fight.

According to pirate historian Charles Johnson:

"...Captain Teach assumed the [name] of Blackbeard, from that large quantity of hair, which like a frightful meteor covered his whole face and frightened America more than any comet *that has appeared for a long time. This beard was black, which he suffered to grow of an extravagant length; as to breadth it came up to his eyes; he was accustomed to twist it with ribbons, in small tails… and turn them around his ears."*

What's more, Blackbeard wore braids in his beard and hair so that it looked like snakes were crawling up his face, and twisted smoking rope into the braids and under his hat to further scare his victims.

Hope he had a bucket of water handy to dunk his head in, if things got too hot!

(nearly)

Verdict: FACT

PIECES OF EIGHT

and other pirate booty

What treasure did a pirate ship capture? Here's a list of the main sources of pirate plunder.

Pieces of eight

Before the days of cash machines, globe-trotting pirates needed money they could spend as easily in Bermuda as they could in Bristol. These coins were usually Spanish "reales," more commonly known as pieces of eight — because if you put eight together you had one silver dollar. Put 16 together and they were worth one doubloon. Following us? Thought not. (There's more information about these sought-after Spanish coins on page 80.)

Jewelry

Capture a ship with passengers on board and you can rob them of their precious rings and watches. Save time with any difficult-to-get-off rings by just chopping off the victim's finger!

18

Maps

What, crumbly bits of old paper?
Believe it or not, maps were
extremely valuable to pirates —
capture a trader's maps and you
could learn all about his trade
routes and set ambushes for
his ships. In fact, maps were so important that pirate
Bartholomew Sharp swapped his maps of the South Seas for
a free pardon from King Charles II back in 1680.

Sugar

In the 1700s, sugar was almost as precious as
gold — a luxury that few could afford. Millions
of slave laborers were forced to work on sugar
plantations in the Caribbean and beyond. Capture a
ship full of sugar heading for Europe and it was like
winning the lottery.

Slaves

Along with sugar plantations, the New World
of North America had huge cotton plantations
that also needed workers. Slave ships took
Africans to America and sold them to work in
the fields. Pirates attacked the slave ships and
sold this human cargo to the highest bidder.

Medicine

Sick pirates were no use to a ship's captain, so medicine was
highly prized. Blackbeard is rumored to have once held a
town for ransom — saying he would kill his captives unless he
received a chest full of pills and potions. His plan worked!

"Black Sam" Bellamy was the unluckiest pirate in history

As a young sailor, Sam Bellamy had his heart broken when the wealthy parents of his sweetheart, Maria Hallett, decided he wasn't good enough (in other words, *rich* enough) for their daughter. Plucky Sam set off to find his fortune, searching for lost treasure in shipwrecks. When the going got tough, however, Bellamy turned to piracy, looting more than 50 ships in the Caribbean and earning the nickname "Black Sam."

I'll be a pirate! Then she'll fancy me.

And the truth is...

In March 1717 Bellamy captured a slave ship, the *Whydah*, collecting a rich booty of gold, silver, ivory and spices. The riches meant that Bellamy could hang up his pirate boots, and he was sailing home to marry young Miss Hallett when his ship was caught in a terrible storm. It sank, killing 144 of its crew — including Bellamy. Awww.

Verdict:  FACT

DAVY JONES' LOCKER

The wreck of the *Whydah* was located in 1984 and became the most famous pirate shipwreck in history. Its booty included:

400 pieces of **Akan gold jewelry**, from West Africa

5,000 kg of **gold dust**

Swords and guns (including "Sun King" pistols, made for Louis XIV of France)

Over 10,000 coins, including:

Escudos from Mexico City

Shillings, crowns, and half-crowns from England

Centimes and sous from France

Reales from Lima, Peru

> ## Pirates sent a "black spot" to people they intended to kill

Want to tell another pirate that you're going to kill him? What could be easier than cutting out a circle of paper, covering it in black ink and then sending it to your intended victim? (OK, yes we can think of a few easier ways too!)

⭐ And the truth is...

Again, this happens in Robert Louis Stevenson's *Treasure Island*, when Billy Bones receives a black spot from his enemies — *but there's no evidence that real pirates did it*. Interesting pirate fact: the idea of the black spot is thought to have come from a tradition among the *real* pirates of the Caribbean of showing an Ace of Spades playing card (traditionally seen as a symbol of death) to a person believed to be a traitor or an informer. The card put the person "on the spot." Clever, eh?

Verdict: PHONY

"AVAST, LANDLUBBERS!"

A guide to pirate lingo

If you want to talk the talk (but not walk the walk), follow our guide to talking like a pirate and you'll be chattering with your shipmates in no time.

NO 3. MEET ME ON THE POOP DECK

Not as smelly as it sounds! The poop deck was the deck that was furthest towards the stern (back) of the boat, and usually above the captain's quarters. The name comes from the French word for stern, la poupe. Its raised position made it ideal for navigation, and for keeping an eye on the crew, which is why the captain positioned himself back there.

Christopher Columbus invented piracy

"In 1492, Columbus sailed the ocean blue..."

You know you're famous when you get a song written about you! And if newspapers had existed in 1492, the Italian explorer, Columbus, would definitely have been front-page news.

OK, he was trying to sail to Japan (by going west instead of east – doh!) but he happened upon something far more valuable – not only the West Indies, but pretty much all of the Central and South American coast, which he naturally claimed for Spain (who were paying him a pretty penny for his services).

No one said that Columbus was the friendly type. On his first voyage he encountered the peace-loving Arawak Indians, took them prisoner, and forced them to show him where they stored their gold. He also took a few back to Spain with him as slaves.

One thing led to another, and not only did he set the slave trade rolling, but he also sparked an interest in trade between Europe and the Americas that saw thousands of vessels crossing the Atlantic, and piracy growing with it.

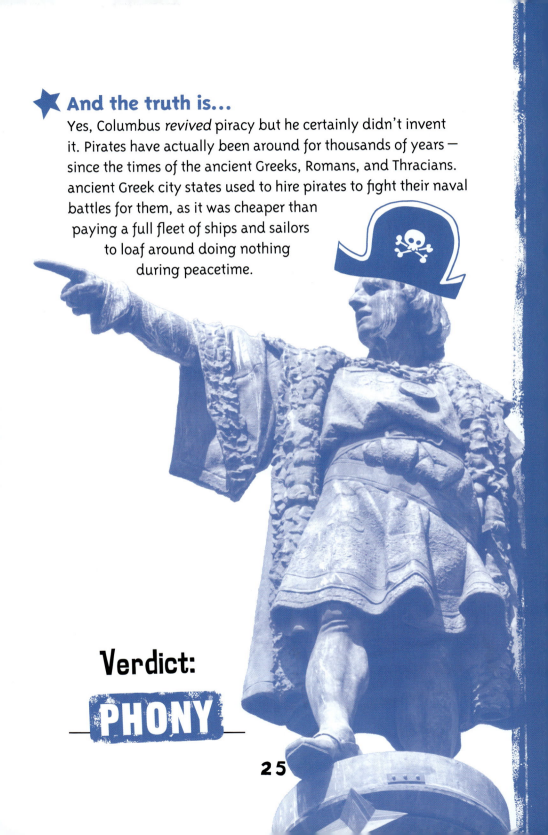

⭐ And the truth is...

Yes, Columbus *revived* piracy but he certainly didn't invent it. Pirates have actually been around for thousands of years — since the times of the ancient Greeks, Romans, and Thracians. ancient Greek city states used to hire pirates to fight their naval battles for them, as it was cheaper than paying a full fleet of ships and sailors to loaf around doing nothing during peacetime.

Verdict:

PHONY

> # Pirates regularly hijacked ships and sold them back to the owners

If you rate pirates by the number of ships they captured, then Black Bart (born plain John Roberts in Casnewydd Bach, Wales) was the LeBron James of the high seas — perched on top of the scoring charts with a mind-boggling 470 ships under his belt (not literally, obviously).

⭐ And the truth is...

Black Bart liked nothing more than hijacking ships and holding them for ransom. He once captured 11 ships in one whopping battle and sold 10 back to their owners. It saved time and made sense! No need to take the ships into port, no need to sell the treasure, and no need to kill the pesky crew. The plan worked well for Bart — until he was killed in a battle with the British Royal Navy. Remember kids, crime never pays.

Verdict: FACT

A pirate once survived a hanging

Hanging was usually about as fatal as a death sentence could get. Dangling from the end of a rope finished off even the roughest and toughest of pirates. So did one really survive it?

 ## And the truth is...

William Duell was hanged at Newgate Prison in 1740. He was cut down and taken away by doctors who were planning to chop him up — until they realized he was still breathing! In two hours he was sitting up, and was soon well enough to be sent back to Newgate. Rather than try and hang him again, "Iron Neck" Duell was eventually transported to America as a prisoner. To his dying day, he claimed he had no memory of being hanged!

Verdict: **FACT** _____

Pirates were all men

Being a pirate was tough — months at sea with no sight of land, a diet of weevil-filled biscuits and rum, and the prospect of death by hanging at the end of it. Not surprisingly, the pirate ranks were swelled by the toughest chaps ever to swing a cutlass — from Blackbeard, Henry Avery and Black Bart, to Calico Jack, Captain Kidd and Sir Henry Morgan.

Let's show 'em what we're made of!

And the truth is...

You might be surprised to hear that two of the most famous pirates ever to set sail were Anne Bonny and Mary Read, who sailed with "Calico Jack" Rackham.

Anne Cormac was born in Ireland, the illegitimate daughter of a lawyer and his housemaid. The family moved to Charleston, South Carolina where the teenager used to dress up as a man and hang around waterfront taverns looking for trouble. In one of those, she met and married sailor John Bonny and moved to the Bahamas. Bonny soon ditched her husband, however, and joined the ship of Calico Jack Rackham.

By coincidence, another female pirate, Mary Read, was aboard the same ship! English-born pirate Read also dressed as a boy from childhood, and even enlisted in the army (as a man!) where she met and married a Dutch soldier. When her husband died, she signed up as a sailor heading for the Caribbean and also found herself aboard Calico Jack's ship.

The cutthroat pair apparently dressed as women on board ship — except when they went into battle — and were every bit as rough and tough as their male shipmates. Rackham and his crew were captured in Jamaica in 1720 and sentenced to hang, but Read and Bonny were spared the noose because they were both pregnant!

 **Verdict:**  **PHONY**

Pirates often killed someone to "guard" their buried treasure

OK, we know that burying treasure wasn't something that happened every day (why bury it when you can spend it?). However, the rumor is that when pirates did get out their spades to hide some stolen loot, they left a fresh corpse (usually of a newly captured prisoner) on top of the treasure chest to frighten away grave robbers — both real and the spook variety (yes, pirates believed in ghosts too!)

⭐ And the truth is...

Well... yes, apparently they did. But there was another reason for leaving a dead body on top of your loot. A mound of freshly dug earth could lead searchers to buried treasure as easily as a big flag saying "Buried treasure here." Put a dead body in there and it looked like a grave — as long as the searchers didn't keep digging!

Verdict: — FACT —

"AVAST, LANDLUBBERS!"

A guide to pirate lingo

If you want to talk the talk (but not walk the walk), follow our guide to talking like a pirate and you'll be chattering with your shipmates in no time.

NO 4. I'LL SEE YOU IN DAVY JONES' LOCKER

Not a cramped locker in a changing room full of smelly old sneakers, but an imaginary place at the bottom of the sea — full of dead people. According to pirate lore, Davy Jones was an evil spirit waiting to escort dead sailors — and pirates — to a watery grave far beneath the waves.

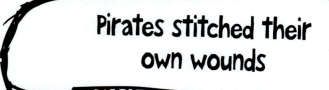

Pirates stitched their own wounds

Pirates were not known for being the prettiest bunch of ocean dwellers. If they weren't toothless (from scurvy) or armless (from a lost duel), they were legless (from rum or battle wounds). But did they really go in for DIY surgery?

⭐ And the truth is...

We have no idea how common it was, but a certain notorious English pirate captain Edward "Ned" Low had his cheek slashed open by a member of his own crew and took offense to the needlework of the ship's doctor. Low killed the doctor and sewed up the cut himself. Not very neatly! The downside: a scary scar. The upside: a scary scar. Perfect for frightening everyone around him.

NED LOW FACT

He once set fire to his own ship's cook because he didn't like the man's food. A pirate Gordon Ramsey!

Verdict: (partly) FACT

Pirate ships had more rats on board than pirates

Rats have long been a problem on board ships. They eat rations, chew through ropes and woodwork, and even attack the cargo if it's edible! The ancient Egyptians hit on the idea of carrying ships' cats over 9,000 years ago to keep the rodents under control.

★ And the truth is...

Pirate ships were no different. One pirate captain reported killing 4,000 rats on just *one* journey across the Atlantic! And a Spanish ship sailing from Europe to South America had daily rat hunts. This might all sound rather hard on the poor rats, but apparently it was kill or be killed — rats often attacked crew members, while an infected rat bite could quickly turn to scabies, a nasty skin condition.

Verdict: **FACT**

The Jolly Roger was originally red

As we already know (see pages 12-13), the traditional pirate flag, known as the Jolly Roger, had a black background with a white skull and crossbones on it. Although a few pirates liked to give it their own individual creative twist, it was always black, wasn't it?

⭐ And the truth is...

Well, no, it wasn't. The French term "joli rouge" (meaning "pretty red") is thought to be the origin of the phrase Jolly Roger (no, it wasn't named after a pirate called Roger...), and red flags were common in naval warfare, signaling that the ships going into battle didn't intend to take any prisoners — in other words, it was a fight to the death. Another theory is that the flag's name comes from "Old Roger" — which is slang for the devil. That's certainly the sort of thing that would, ahem, float a pirate's boat!

Verdict: **FACT**

THE TOP 10 HIGHEST EARNING PIRATES

PIRATES WERE IN IT FOR THE LOOT, SO WHO WERE THE MOST SUCCESSFUL AT GRABBING THE BOOTY?

#	Pirate	Earnings
1	Samuel "Black Sam" Bellamy	$146m
2	Sir Francis Drake	$140m
3	Thomas Tew	$124m
4	Bartholomew "Black Bart" Roberts	$100m
5	John Bowen	$48m
6	Jean Fleury	$38m
7	Thomas White	$19m
8	John Halsey	$16m
9	Harry Morgan	$16m
10	Edward "Blackbeard" Teach	$15m

Based on estimated earnings. Research carried out in 2008.

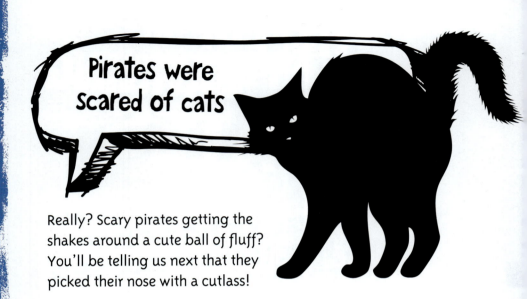

Pirates were scared of cats

Really? Scary pirates getting the shakes around a cute ball of fluff? You'll be telling us next that they picked their nose with a cutlass!

⭐ And the truth is...

Pirates often kept animals on board ship. Buccaneers kept hunting dogs, and many ships carried cats and even monkeys. But pirate crews were very superstitious, and had rules to go with the cats as follows:

⭐ If a black cat walks towards a sailor he will be lucky.

⭐ If a black cat walks towards a sailor but then turns around and walks away he will be unlucky.

⭐ If a black cat is thrown overboard a storm will follow and the ship will be cursed.

(Wouldn't it be safer to just make sure the ship's cat wasn't black?)

Verdict: FACT

"AVAST, LANDLUBBERS!"

A guide to pirate lingo

If you want to talk the talk (but not walk the walk), follow our guide to talking like a pirate and you'll be chattering with your shipmates in no time.

NO 5. IT'S JUNK AND CACKLE FRUIT FOR DINNER AGAIN

Where to start with this one? Junk was a pirate term for salted beef or pork. Salt was commonly used to preserve meat and make it last on long journeys. It had the unfortunate side effect of making the meat really hard — not great if, like a lot of pirates, you were missing a few teeth. Cackle fruit was a term used for chicken's eggs. We have no idea why, but we might start using it ourselves. "Cackle fruit on toast for breakfast, please!"

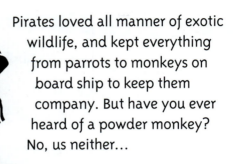

Pirates kept "powder monkeys" on their ships

Pirates loved all manner of exotic wildlife, and kept everything from parrots to monkeys on board ship to keep them company. But have you ever heard of a powder monkey? No, us neither...

⭐ And the truth is...

A "powder monkey" was slang for the person whose job it was to keep the pirate gunners supplied with gunpowder. They went back and forth between the powder magazine in the ship's hold (in other words, the place where the gunpowder was kept), to all the guns on board ship. It was usually a young boy aged 12-14 who landed the job. As you'd expect on a pirate ship, the boys were often kidnapped and forced to work against their will. They weren't old enough to fight but the pirates still managed to find a use for them. Ingenious!

Verdict:  FACT

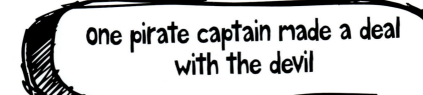

one pirate captain made a deal with the devil

William Lewis' feats in the early 1700s are legendary. For a decade he sailed the Caribbean capturing one ship after another, and often cheating death. Sentenced to hanging in Havana, Cuba, he escaped in a canoe, and began stealing ships — each one larger than the last — until he ended up with a fully armed warship with a crew of 50!

⭐ And the truth is...

Lewis' luck finally ran out in 1727. He was chasing a rich treasure ship off the Carolina coast, but couldn't match it for speed. That is, until he climbed the mast and started pulling out his own hair and shouting, "Good devil — take this until we meet..." His ship caught the treasure ship, but that night his terrified crew crept into his room and shot him to death in his sleep!

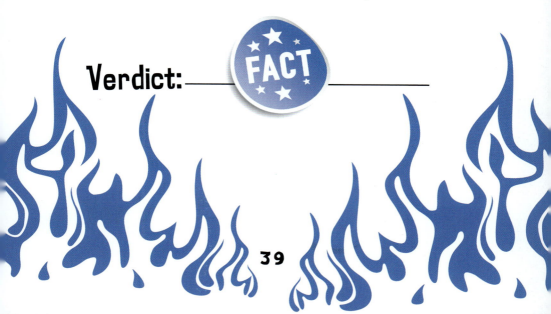

Verdict: ——— FACT ———

The most successful pirate ever was never caught

Born in Wales in 1682 as plain old John Roberts (the name Black Bart was only used *after* his death), it's believed our would-be pirate changed his name to Bartholomew after the well-known buccaneer Bartholomew Sharp. Roberts went to sea when he was a fresh-faced 13-year-old and worked on slave ships traveling between West Africa and the Americas. In 1719, his ship was captured by pirates led by fellow Welshman Howell Davis, and Roberts and many of his fellow crew members were given a choice — piracy or death. Mmm, let me think about that one for a minute....

Roberts took to his new profession like a pirate to water, and when Davis was killed in a gun battle on the island of Príncipe, the young man was elected captain — just six weeks after coming aboard!

Roberts quickly earned a reputation as a fearless — and successful — pirate. He hit the jackpot when he ran across a fleet of 42 Portuguese ships with no military escort off the Brazilian coast. He had soon captured the richest ship in the fleet, which was overflowing with 40,000 gold coins and jewelry designed for the King of Portugal himself.

And the truth is...

 During his lifetime, Roberts captured over 400 ships and took £50 million ($77.5 million) worth of pirate loot in today's money! He was the most feared and admired pirate of his day, and robbed everything that sailed in or out of the West Indies — almost bringing trade in the area to a standstill. He was eventually killed in 1722 in a battle with an English warship HMS *Swallow*, and was thrown overboard by his crew so his body couldn't be captured by the English.

Verdict:

PIRATE PUNISHMENTS

OUCH!

It was great being a pirate! Until you got caught... Here's what you could expect as a punishment. Best read from behind your fingers.

HANGING

Most pirates who were caught were hanged — it was slow and gruesome, and as they were hanged in public it was supposed to put off other would-be pirates from following in their footsteps. In reality, it was more like a spectator sport. In London, pirates were hanged at Execution Docks, so the sailors could watch and enjoy it.

Believe it or not, pirates were most scared of hanging because they believed that without a proper burial, their spirits would suffer eternally. Big softies.

GIBBETING

Fancy a bit of sunbathing? Um, think again. At Dead Man's Cay in Jamaica, pirates were executed by being locked in an iron cage (a gibbet) and stayed there until they died of dehydration. Pirate skeletons stayed in these cages — sometimes for years — as a deterrent to others.

BURIED FACEDOWN

You might think being dead was the end of the story. Oh no, it could get worse! Pirates were often buried facedown — the ultimate punishment as it meant your soul was lost forever. Even though they terrorized the seas, pirates still hoped to go to heaven. Fat chance of that!

DEATH OF A THOUSAND CUTS

Famous Chinese pirate Cheng Chih-lung suffered this gruesome fate, along with his two sons. As it sounds, the executioner made cuts to the arms, legs and torso of a victim, before cutting bits off — ears, toes, etc. As well as being unbearably painful, it also meant the victim wouldn't be whole in the afterlife.

Blackbeard had 14 wives

As we've learned, Blackbeard was a larger-than-life character, surrounded by myth, falsehood and what we technically like to call fibs. So what about the story that he had 14 wives? Is this real or a tall tale?

⭐ And the truth is...

We don't know if Blackbeard loved tying the knot, or if — like many of his myths — this is make-believe. One thing we do know for sure, though, is that his last wife was Mary Ormond (or possibly Ormand) of Bath, North Carolina. The daughter of a wealthy plantation owner, she met and married the pirate when she was just 16!

Their wedding was quite the society affair — attended by Royal Governor Charles Eden. Unfortunately, Blackbeard wasn't the stay-at-home type — he left young Mary in port in 1718 and never returned. He couldn't, he was dead! Her ghost is said to roam the cliff tops waiting for his ship. Which is kind of sweet when you think about it.

Verdict: (probably) PHONY

"AVAST, LANDLUBBERS!"

A guide to pirate lingo

If you want to talk the talk (but not walk the walk), follow our guide to talking like a pirate and you'll be chattering with your shipmates in no time.

NO 6. I'M TAKING A CAULK THIS AFTERNOON

The gaps between the wooden planks on a ship's deck were sealed with oakum — basically bits of old rope covered in tar and then "caulked" (that's stuffed, to you and me) into the gaps. Lie down on the deck and you would find yourself as stripy as a pirate zebra. Any pirate planning to have a crafty nap on deck would tell his shipmates he was "taking a caulk."

Pirates sometimes dressed as women to attract passing ships

There's no easier way of capturing a ship than by getting yourself invited on board. A quick skirmish to overpower the crew, and the cargo is yours. No tiresome sea chases, no risk of damage to the vessel from cannonballs and grappling hooks, and all your crew still in one piece to fight another day. But how could a bunch of fearsome-looking pirates hope to have the red carpet rolled out for them by a merchant ship swelling with booty? A famous painting by French artist Auguste-Francois Biard shows a group of pirates dressed as women capturing a ship. So is this how they did it — by acting like a group of damsels in distress?

 And the truth is...

It's a great idea, but there is no evidence that it's fact rather than (visual) fiction. We reckon if it had happened, someone would have written about it — not just painted a picture.

Verdict: (probably) **PHONY**

46

The Greeks invented the word "pirate"

The brainy ancient Greeks invented everything from the Olympics to steam power to prime numbers. So who would bet against them inventing the word "pirate"? Not us!

⭐ And the truth is...

Sure enough, the word pirate comes from the Greek "peiran" meaning "to attempt" or "to attack." The Romans then tweaked the word to "pirata," which meant piracy. The Greeks were also at the forefront of some of the most horrible pirate punishments, and are thought to have invented "keelhauling," which is dragging a seaman under the ship from bow to stern (that's front to back, to you and me). For sheer gruesomeness, this was matched only by the Carthaginians, who came up with the idea of tying a living man to a corpse, and throwing the pair overboard. Who'd want to upset the Carthaginians? Not us!

Verdict: **FACT**

"AVAST, LANDLUBBERS!"

A guide to pirate lingo

If you want to talk the talk (but not walk the walk), follow our guide to talking like a pirate and you'll be chattering with your shipmates in no time.

NO 7. BRING ME MY BLACK JACK, WE'RE DRINKING SOME GROG

As you can imagine, pirates preferred alcohol to tea and biscuits. Grog was one of the most common names for a favorite pirate drink, which was traditionally made from water, rum, and weak beer, and named after British Vice Admiral Edward Vernon, who introduced the drink to the Royal Navy in August 1740. Why grog? Because Vernon wore a coat made from grogram cloth (silk mixed with wool) and was nicknamed Old Grog. Black Jacks were large leather cups, strengthened with a coating of tar.

Roman Emperor Pompey killed 10,000 pirates

As we've discovered, pirates have been around for thousands of years. Back in the days of the Roman Empire, pirate mercenaries from Cilicia, in Asia Minor, were patrolling the Mediterranean, robbing Roman trading vessels, preventing trade between cities in the Empire, and kidnapping local officials. So what did the Romans do about it?

⭐ And the truth is...

The Romans weren't about to take any threat to the smooth running of their Empire sitting down! In 67 BCE, Emperor Pompey was granted special powers to clear the Mediterranean of pirates. He took his job very seriously, destroying 1,300 ships, taking 20,000 prisoners and killing 10,000 pirates — all within three months!

Verdict:

FACT

Julius Caesar was once captured by pirates

Sometimes a ship's passengers were as valuable as its cargo, with rich and important people often targeted for kidnap and ransom. So did the great Roman emperor ever fall victim to a cutthroat pirate crew?

 And the truth is...

He did indeed! A 25-year-old Caesar was sailing the Aegean Sea in 78 BCE when he was captured by Sicilian pirates. The pirates wanted to ask for a ransom of 20 talents of silver (around $623,000 in today's money), but Caesar demanded they ask for 50 talents — a sum far more suited to his importance! Caesar was held for six weeks before his ransom was paid. After his release, he gathered together his own fleet, tracked the pirates down and had them crucified. You don't mess with Caesar.

Verdict:

FACT

PIRATE OR PRIVATEER?

Throughout history there have been many different kinds of pirates, with lots of different names. Here's a list of the most interesting:

PIRATE

The most common term for someone who robs ships at sea. Comes from the Latin word "pirata" (page 48). The word was first used by the Greek historian Polybius around 140 BCE.

VIKINGS

Believe it or not, "viking" means "pirate men," and when the Roman Empire came to an end, it was the Vikings from Norway, Sweden, and Denmark who ruled the waves. They sailed the seas from the 8th to 11th centuries in long ships called longships (doh!), robbing, pillaging, and generally being unpleasant. That's pirates for you!

PRIVATEER

Ships' captains who were given a special license, called a Letter of Marque, to attack and capture other ships on behalf of their own country. Privateers often turned to piracy themselves, however, when they discovered how much pirates could earn compared to their own salaries!

CORSAIR

A French word (meaning "chaser") for a French sailor or privateer who sailed mainly in the Mediterranean.

BARBARY PIRATES

A group of pirates who attacked ships off the Barbary Coast (North Africa, to you and me). From 1569-1616, nearly 500 English ships were captured by Barbary pirates. They were so successful that they set up their own pirate empire, the Barbary States, with its own government!

BUCCANEERS

When the Spanish government chased the Dutch, English, and French settlers off the island of Hispaniola in the Caribbean, they made the island of Tortuga their home and began to attack Spanish shipping. Well, wouldn't you?

The island of Madagascar was once ruled by pirates

The land of cuddly lemurs a hideout for pirates? That sounds even less likely than four talking animals from Central Park Zoo crash-landing there and learning how to live in the wild.

⭐ And the truth is...

The island's location made a great stopover for pirates planning to plunder ships in the Indian Ocean. By the late 17th century, a base had been established there by Adam Baldridge, a former buccaneer from Jamaica. Baldridge went from piracy to daylight robbery — selling wine and other provisions to pirate crews at massively inflated prices. For example, he would buy a barrel of wine for $30 in America and sell it for $467 on Madagascar!

How much? That's daylight robbery!

Not surprisingly, a small number of enterprising pirates set up as unofficial rulers on the island and founded their own colonies, including "King Samuel" (Abraham Samuel) and the most successful, John Plantain, who called himself "King of Ranter Bay," and eventually became ruler of the whole island.

Verdict: ────────

Francis Drake was a pirate

Vice Admiral Drake was one of the most famous Englishmen of his time. He completed only the second circumnavigation of the globe (that means sailing completely around the world) between 1577–80, for which he was knighted, and then helped the English fleet kick the behinds of the Spanish Armada in 1588. And now you're telling us he did all this with a parrot on his shoulder and a peg leg? Arrr, it can't be true!

And the truth is...

Well, it all depends which side you are on!

By the mid 16th century, Spain and Portugal were the world's main superpowers, and were stinking rich with all the loot they were plundering from the New World (North, South, and Central America). France and England decided to get in on the act and Drake — with the full support of Queen Elizabeth I — helped himself to the booty from several Spanish galleons. And paid some into the Queen's own bank account, of course.

His richest capture was the *Cacafuego*, a galleon that contained, according to reports, "13 chests full of *reales of plate* [silver coins], four score [80] pound weight of gold, and six and 20 tons of [uncoined] silver." Not bad for a day's work.

A hero to the English he might have been, but King Philip II of Spain definitely viewed *El Draque* as a pirate and offered a reward of 20,000 ducats (around $6 million in today's money) for his life. The Spanish never got their hands on him, though — Drake died of dysentery in 1596 during an attack on San Juan in Puerto Rico.

DRAKE FACT

For all his heroic actions, Drake also had a dark and unpleasant secret - he was one of the first English traders to sell African slaves to the Spanish plantations in the Caribbean.

Verdict: —————— FACT ——————

A TASTE OF THE "CAT"

OUCH!

How did pirates punish their shipmates and torture prisoners – from the cat o' nine tails to keelhauling and slicing off ears!

KEELHAULING

The nasty — not to say painful — practice of tying ropes to a sailor and then dragging him under the keel of the ship (that's the bottom, to you and me) from front to back. Do it quickly and the unfortunate victim could suffer severe cuts at best, and might even lose limbs or his head to the razor-sharp barnacles stuck to the hull. Do it slowly and he might miss the barnacles but end up drowning. Not much of a choice, really.

CAT O' NINE TAILS

The naval cat — also known as the captain's daughter — was a whip made of nine knotted strands of thick cord attached to a wooden handle. It was designed to cut into the flesh of its victim and cause permanent scarring. If you were really unlucky, you caught blood poisoning and died from the dirty, bacteria-infested rope that had been used on countless unfortunate victims before you!

BURNING BODY PARTS

English pirate Ned Low was a short-tempered bully who usually drew his cutlass first and asked questions later. On one occasion, faced with a prisoner who wouldn't tell him the whereabouts of some treasure, Low tied the man's hands behind his back, weaved rope between his fingers, and set light to it — burning the poor man's hands down to the bone.

NEEDLE AND THREAD

Dutch pirate Dirk Chivers is said to have sewed a ship captain's mouth shut with a needle and thread to stop his complaining! Bet the captain was lost for words.

MAROONING

Any pirate who stole from his shipmates, or deserted his post in battle, was likely to be abandoned on a desert island with nothing but a bottle of water, a loaded pistol and the clothes he stood up in. The unfortunate fellow might starve, die of thirst, drown or be eaten by sharks. If he decided to shoot himself, his soul would never make it to heaven!

Captain Kidd was employed by the British government

I demand to speak to my MP!

William Kidd was a Scottish sailor who was hanged for piracy at Execution Dock in Wapping, London in 1710. Kidd must have thought his luck was in when the rope snapped during his execution. Unfortunately for him, another rope was quickly found and he was hanged a second time! His body was then tied to a post at the water's edge until the tide had washed over it three times. It was then covered head to toe in tar, and hung in a cage as a deterrent to other pirates (well, wouldn't it put you off?). So, we ask you, is that any way to treat an employee of His Majesty's government?

And the truth is...

Born in Dundee, the son of a vicar, William Kidd was a perfectly respectable sea captain for much of his career. In fact, during the wars against France, he helped to protect English shipping in the Caribbean against French raids.

In 1695, Kidd accepted a Royal Commission to hunt down pirates in the Indian Ocean — the reward was a share of any loot he captured. But that's when things started to go wrong. Firstly, a Royal Navy ship took half of his crew to fight for king and country, and Kidd was forced to replace them with corsairs. When Kidd's ship failed to land as much loot as they had hoped, the crew turned mutinous, and Kidd bashed one of them on the head with a bucket and killed him.

Pressured by his crew into attacking some smaller ships, the word spread back to Britain that Kidd was a pirate-hunter turned pirate. Ironically, his greatest success as a "pirate," the capture of the *Quedagh Merchant* in 1698 — a ship full-to-bursting with gold, jewels and precious silks — was more or less part of what he had been instructed to do by the British government. The *Quedagh's* captain was English, but the cargo was bound for Armenia and the ship was sailing with French papers.

Nevertheless, back in England, the government bowed to political pressure to make good on its promises to stamp out piracy and made an example of Kidd, hanging him. Twice.

Verdict:

The most feared pirate in China was a woman

Chinese pirates ruled the waterways of Southeast Asia for nearly 2,000 years — robbing merchant ships and waging war on towns and villages. When Europe started to establish empires in the region in the 16th and 17th centuries, the situation got worse — there was even more to rob! So did a female pirate really become the baddest cutthroat of the South China Seas?

And the truth is...

You'd better believe it! Ching Shih (also known as Zheng Shi, meaning "widow Zheng") lived during the 19th century and, as legend has it, was captured by pirate chief Zheng Yi, who wanted to make her his wife. Ching agreed — as long as she could be joint leader of his pirate fleet and keep half his share of any loot they captured together!

Over the next six years, they built a powerful pirate navy with six color-coded fleets, led by their own "Red Flag Fleet," supported by black, white, blue, yellow, and green fleets — like handy pirate reserve teams.

When Zheng Yi died, Ching became the undisputed big boss, and took control of the entire fleet of an estimated 400-1,200 ships, and 50,000-70,000 pirates. Over ten years, Ching sailed the coast of Imperial China, fighting, robbing, and getting rich. When the Chinese government decided to take her on, Ching captured 63 of their ships and gave the sailors a choice — join us or die! Not surprisingly, most joined!

Knowing they couldn't beat her, the Chinese emperor finally offered Ching an amnesty — she could keep all her money and a small fleet of ships as long as she retired from piracy. Ching accepted and set up a successful casino that she ran until her death, at the ripe old age of 69. One of the few pirates to die of old age!

Verdict: **FACT**

Pirates mixed gunpowder and rum!

Pirates and rum go together like fish and chips, but what's this rumor about pirates mixing rum with gunpowder? That sounds like a disaster about to happen! So what's the real story?

⭐ And the truth is...

Dangerous as it sounds, pirates — and even British Royal Navy sailors — used to test the strength of rum by mixing it with gunpowder and then setting light to it. Only rum that wasn't too watered down would light up. The flame was considered the "proof" of the alcohol content, and only a keg or bottle with sufficient "proof" was purchasable. This is where the current system of measuring alcohol's strength and referring to it as, for example, 75% proof comes from. See, you learn something new every day.

Verdict: ──── **FACT** ────

"AVAST, LANDLUBBERS!"

A guide to pirate lingo

If you want to talk the talk (but not walk the walk), follow our guide to talking like a pirate and you'll be chattering with your shipmates in no time.

NO 8. HE'S A SCURVY KNAVE, AND NO MISTAKE

Scurvy was a common disease among pirates and honest sailors alike. A lack of fresh fruit and vegetables, and a diet of salted meat, caused many seafarers to suffer from scabby skin, wobbly teeth, a bleeding nose, and generally 'orrible yellow skin. A knave is a crafty or untrustworthy person. Put the two together, and it's not someone you'd want to rub shoulders with — or anything else for that matter!

The pirates of the Caribbean started out hunting pigs

Jack Sparrow, Captain Barbossa, and the rest of the *Black Pearl's* crew have made the pirates of the Caribbean some of the best-known swashbucklers on the planet. OK, we know they're not real, but it's kind of based on real people, right? So what's all this about hunting pigs not treasure?

★ And the truth is...

The earliest settlers in the Caribbean — specifically on the island of Hispaniola — weren't pirates, they were naval deserters, castaways, escaped prisoners, or runaway slaves. Most came from England, France and Holland, but there were lots of other nationalities represented.

These settlers made a living as huntsmen and traders, killing the wild animals on the island and trading the meat and skins for guns, ammunition, and rum. The name buccaneer in fact comes from the Arawak Indian word "buccan," a wooden frame for smoking meat. French hunters with a taste for the local cattle and pigs adopted the term "boucanier," which in time became buccaneer.

Although they were a rowdy bunch, these buccaneers might have lived happily ever after on their island, if the Spanish authorities hadn't decided to drive them off. The buccaneers moved their base to Tortuga, off the coast of Hispaniola, and in retaliation began to attack Spanish shipping. At first they only had large canoes called "piraguas," but thanks to their highly developed hunting skills they had soon stolen larger ships — and developed a taste for piracy into the bargain!

One of their first leaders was a Frenchman called Jean le Vasseur, an exiled military engineer who planned and built a powerful stronghold around Tortuga's main harbor to prevent attacks. The buccaneers' fearsome reputation led to offers of work as privateers from Spain's main rivals, and before you knew it — the hunters of Hispaniola had become the pirates of the Caribbean!

Verdict:

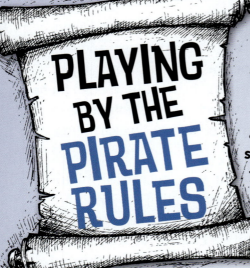

PLAYING BY THE PIRATE RULES

Believe it or not, pirates lived by a set of rules called "The Pirate Articles," which were drawn up by notorious Welsh pirate Bartholomew Roberts (aka Black Bart) and his crew in 1719. Pirates swore on the Bible to uphold the articles, and were even known to kill men who refused to sign!

From "Lights and candles shall be put out at eight o'clock every night" to "There shall be no fighting aboard ship..." here they are (we have rewritten some of them in easier-to-understand English):

 Lights and candles shall be put out at eight o'clock every night. If any crew members want to drink after that time, they must sit on the deck and do so without lights.

 Every man shall keep his cutlass and pistol clean and ready for use at all times.

 No one shall play cards or dice for money.

 No boys or women are allowed on board. Any man who brings a woman on board (disguised as a man) will be put to death.

All men shall share equally in the division of treasure. Any man found taking more than his fair share shall be marooned. Any man found robbing another man will have his nose and ears split, and then be marooned (tough!).

Any man who deserts the ship or leaves his position during a battle will be put to death or marooned.

There shall be no fighting aboard ship. Any quarrels shall be settled on shore by a duel with swords or pistols.

Every crew member gets an equal vote on the ship's actions, and an equal share of food and drink on board ship.

The captain and the quartermaster (usually a captain's second-in-command) will receive two men's share of any treasure. All other officers get one-and-a-quarter share.

Any man who loses a limb in service of his ship will receive 800 pieces of eight (less for losing a finger, and so on...).

Musicians on board ship have Sundays off(!).

François L'ollonais ate the heart of one of his victims

French pirate L'Ollonais got his nickname from his hometown of Les Sables d'Olonne in Brittany (L'Ollonais roughly translates as "from Olonne"). He arrived in the Caribbean as a servant, but soon joined up with the buccaneers and found he had a talent for piracy. In 1667, he captured a Spanish treasure ship carrying a whopping 40,000 pieces of eight, as well as a hold full of precious jewelry.

★ And the truth is...

The Spanish feared L'Ollonais as much for his extreme cruelty as his skills as a pirate. He often chopped off the limbs of victims who didn't give up their valuables quickly enough, and once cut out the heart of a Spanish sailor he had captured — and ate it in front of his men! L'Ollonais met a messy fate himself when he was captured and killed by a tribe of Native Americans.

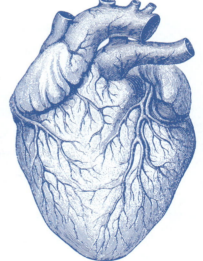

Verdict:

The youngest pirate was nine years old

Historians tell us that teenage pirates were common in the early 18th century, as captured teens often joined their captors on the wrong side of the law. But did ships really employ boys not yet out of short trousers?

 ### And the truth is...

According to a report by one Abijah Savage from 1716, his ship was captured by pirate Sam Bellamy and his crew off the coast of Antigua. A young passenger, John King, believed to be around nine, waved his parents goodbye and willingly joined the pirates. Sadly, King's pirate life was cut short when Bellamy's ship the *Whydah* sank (see pages 20-21). Divers examining the wreck 300 years later found a small shoe and a short leg bone believed to belong to King. Sounds convincing to us!

Verdict: (probably) FACT

71

Blackbeard shot one of his own crew for a joke

Pirates had a strange sense of humor, and Blackbeard was one of the strangest. On board ship, he would often create his own version of hell, by filling the hold with brimstone, setting light to it, and challenging his men to withstand the suffocating fumes longer than he could. No one ever beat him.

★ And the truth is...

While drinking with one of his crew, Israel Hands, Blackbeard fired two pistols under the table into Hands' knees, crippling him. Blackbeard explained to his crew afterwards, "If I didn't kill one of you now and again, you'd forget who I was," Erm, no, they wouldn't — you've got a black beard!

Verdict:

PIRATE NICKNAMES

Calico Jack, Blackbeard, and other great pirate nicknames!

Nickname	Real name	Nationality
Blackbeard	Edward Teach	English
Black Sam	Samuel Bellamy	English
Black Bart	Bartholomew Roberts	Welsh
Calico Jack	John Rackham	English
Diabolito (Little Devil)	Unknown	Cuban
Black Caesar	Unknown	West African
Exterminator	Daniel Montbars	French
Simon the Dancer	Seiment Danziger	Dutch
Red Legs Greaves	Unknown	Scottish
Le Lyonnais	Jacques Tavernier	French

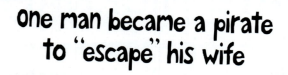

One man became a pirate to "escape" his wife

It was claimed by historian Captain Johnson, who wrote a famous book on pirates, that Stede Bonnet, a wealthy landowner from Barbados who was sometimes called "The Gentleman Pirate," took to piracy to escape his wife. Ooh, just wait until she hears about that!

⭐ And the truth is...

Historians report that marital problems *were* one of the reasons that Bonnet turned to piracy. Whatever the truth, we do know that Bonnet gave up a comfortable lifestyle and found fame and fortune as a pirate, even teaming up with Blackbeard for joint attacks. Of course, it all ended badly. Bonnet was eventually captured and hanged along with 29 members of his crew.

PIRATE FACT

Bonnet pleaded for the amputation of all his limbs instead of hanging.

Verdict: (partly) **FACT**

"AVAST, LANDLUBBERS!"

A guide to pirate lingo

If you want to talk the talk (but not walk the walk), follow our guide to talking like a pirate and you'll be chattering with your shipmates in no time.

NO 9. YOU'LL MAKE A GOOD SWABBIE, YOU LANDLUBBER

A swab was a ship's mop made of the ends of old rope. So a swabbie was the person with the job of mopping the ship's deck. Not so bad, was it? Mmm, imagine having to clean up all the blood and guts after a major fight and you might change your mind! A lubber was a clumsy person, so a landlubber was someone who was more comfortable on land.

Robinson Crusoe was rescued by a pirate

Alexander Selkirk was a real-life Scottish buccaneer who, in 1704, asked to be left on the tiny, uninhabited island of Más a Tierra off the coast of Chile rather than set sail in what he considered to be an unseaworthy ship. Selkirk's hunch was correct — the *Cinque Ports* sank off the coast of Colombia and the surviving crew members were forced to surrender to the Spanish.

★ And the truth is...

Selkirk hadn't considered the downside — more than four years stranded on the island with nothing but wild goats to eat! As luck would have it, he was rescued in 1709 by the explorer — and sometime buccaneer — William Dampier. Selkirk's story made him famous, and inspired Daniel Defoe to write *Robinson Crusoe* in 1719. So far so good: but it wasn't Robinson Crusoe who was rescued by a pirate, it was Alexander Selkirk!

Verdict:  **PHONY**

WHERE IN THE WORLD?

Five uninhabited islands you've never heard of:

 ### OKUNOSHIMA ISLAND

Just 1.9 miles (3 km) off the coast of Japan, Okunoshima is home to nothing but rabbits. Why? Because it was once the site of a chemical weapons plant, producing poison gas for the Japanese Imperial Army from 1929-45.

Robinson Crusoe rating: 1/10

 ### ANTIPODES ISLANDS

A group of volcanic islands south of New Zealand. Cold, desolate and a downright harsh place to survive. Two sailors were shipwrecked there and died as recently as 1999.

Robinson Crusoe rating: 3/10

 ### JACO ISLAND

Off the coast of East Timor, between Indonesia and Australia, Jaco Island is uninhabited because it's considered by locals to be sacred land. Tourists are allowed to visit, though, and local fishermen act as tour guides. Sounds really rather welcoming.

Robinson Crusoe rating: 8/10

 ### CLIPPERTON ISLAND

A coral atoll (a ring-shaped coral reef with a lagoon in the middle) in the Pacific Ocean, Clipperton used to be home to a British company mining bird and bat poo (don't laugh, it makes great fertilizer!) but they left the island in 1917, leaving just the birds, the bats and the poo.

Robinson Crusoe rating: 5/10

 ### NORTH BROTHER ISLAND

An island in the East River in New York City, this is a protected bird nesting area that is off limits to the public. Probably just as well - locals claim it's haunted by the ghosts of typhoid victims who stayed in the hospital on the island, which was closed in 1942. Spooky.

Robinson Crusoe rating: 4/10

PIRATE PROVISIONS...

BLURGH!

What did pirates like to get their teeth into? Here's a list of our favorite pirate grub, from dough-boys to salmagundi.

BUMBO

A drink made from rum mixed with spices and cane syrup.

DOUGH-BOYS

Boiled dumplings — often cooked in seawater to avoid wasting precious drinking water. Yuck!

FLIP

A warm drink made from beer, rum, and sugar.

GROG

Watered-down rum (see page 49).

PICKLED SHARK

As you can imagine, fish was a large part of a pirate's diet. Any fish that could be pickled and preserved for long journeys was used, although shark sounds pretty unappetizing. However, it was the favorite dish of William Dampier, who liked it with pepper and vinegar!

SALMAGUNDI

A spicy stew made from minced meat or fish that was soaked in wine (so far, so delicious) and then mixed with just about anything that the ship's cook had hanging around — from hard-boiled eggs to anchovies, pickled vegetables or cabbage! In England, the stew became known as "solomon-gundy" and is thought to have inspired the nursery rhyme "Solomon Grundy."

SHIP'S BISCUITS/HARDTACK

Designed to last through months-long journeys, these were rock hard and often inhabited by black-headed weevils (a type of bug). For a treat, pirates mixed the biscuits with bacon grease to make a sticky mess called skillygalee. Yum!

TOBACCO

Regarded by pirates as one of the most important parts of their provisions, tobacco was usually smoked in long-handled clay pipes and was used to keep extreme hunger pangs at bay.

TURTLES

Caribbean pirates considered the meat of the sea tortoise (turtle, to you and me) a real delicacy. Better still, the animals could be kept alive in the ship's hold, so the meat would be fresh. What did it taste like? According to one pirate, "The flesh... eats much like choice veal, but the fat is of a green color." Beats skillygalee, we suppose.

"Pieces of eight" were invented by Robert Louis Stevenson

Treasure Island, Stevenson's tale of "buccaneers and buried gold," published in 1883, made landlubbers around the world believe in one-legged pirates and treasure maps marked with an X. Some of it was based on fact, some of it purely fiction!

⭐ And the truth is...

Although Stevenson invented many a pirate myth now believed to be true, Long John Silver's parrot was actually squawking about a real coin (see pages 18-19). The Spanish dollar or peso was the universal currency of Caribbean pirates (like the Euro, but worth more). It bore the number 8 on it and — this is the clever bit — could be cut into eight pieces in order to provide small change. In case you needed to pay for a pirate parking meter at the harbor!

Verdict: PHONY

Pirates loved to wear fancy clothes

I love my new coat - don't you?

Thieving cutthroats with peg legs and cutlasses between their teeth: that's how we think of pirates. But were they really fashion models in the making?

⭐ And the truth is...

Yes, gold and jewels made pirates rich, but they also liked nothing more than to steal fancy clothes from their victims and wear them — even if they didn't fit. "Calico Jack" Rackham was so-called because of his taste for flashy cotton trousers, and little-known English pirate Kit Oloard wore "black velvet trousers and jackets, crimson silk socks, black felt hat, brown beard, and shirt collar embroidered in black silk" according to one pirate historian. Pirates liked the idea of dressing like gentlemen, but not *acting* like gentlemen!

Verdict:  FACT

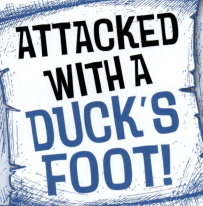

ATTACKED WITH A DUCK'S FOOT!

Pirates carried all sorts of weird and wacky weapons! From a cutlass to a tar bomb - here's the pirates' arsenal explored:

CUTLASS

The ultimate pirate sword was curved not straight. Why? So it didn't get tangled up in all those pesky ropes they have on ships to hold the sails up. Smart.

BRASS KNIFE

Salt water rusted iron and steel knives but brass knives stayed sharp and shiny. It was more important that they were sharp than shiny, of course.

AX

Short, light axes were used for chopping the ropes that held up sails. And if a ship couldn't sail away it was a sitting duck — sorry, ship.

TAR BOMB

Stick a ball of tar to the end of a rope, set it on fire, and throw it onto the deck of your enemy's ship. They can't pull it off because the tar sticks to the deck like chewing gum in your hair. While the crew is busy trying to put out the fire, you jump aboard and capture their boat. *Evil laugh*

FLINTLOCK PISTOL

A noisy, unreliable pistol used by Caribbean pirates, the flintlock took a long time to load and often failed to fire at all. No wonder Blackbeard kept a dozen of them in his belt at all times. If they failed to fire, he could at least throw them!

GRAPPLING HOOK

If you wanted to board an enemy ship, you needed one of these — a three-headed hook attached to a length of rope. It wasn't sophisticated, but it was effective. The hooks dug into a boat's wooden hull and couldn't be pried loose — firmly attaching the pirate ship to its prey.

BUCCANEER KNIVES

These were long, sharp knives — somewhere between a cutlass and a machete (a mutlass?) — that were used mainly for hunting pigs in the Caribbean. They could also be used on, oink, troublesome people.

DUCK'S FOOT

Want to shoot someone, but worried you might not hit them? Use a duck's foot — a gun with four barrels! The barrels were joined together side by side and looked like — you've guessed it — a duck's foot. Think about it.

Captain Hook was based on J.M. Barrie's postman

We all know the story of *Peter Pan* — the boy who never grew up — and his battles with the villainous Captain Hook. But did you know that the *Peter Pan* author plucked the devilish pirate from real life?

Don't suppose you need a letter opener?

⭐ And the truth is...

Barrie's famous pirate took his name from Hooky Crewe, a postman in Barrie's home town of Angus, Scotland, who had lost his right hand and replaced it with an iron hook. However, the author admits that some of the more malicious aspects of Captain Hook's character came from one of his teachers!

FACT (partly)

Verdict: ⎯⎯⎯⎯⎯⎯⎯⎯⎯

"AVAST, LANDLUBBERS!"

A guide to pirate lingo

If you want to talk the talk (but not walk the walk), follow our guide to talking like a pirate and you'll be chattering with your shipmates in no time.

NO 10. HE'S A TASTY SWASHER, AND NO MISTAKE

A swasher, or swashbuckler, refers to a particular kind of fighting man, and is a term dating back to the 16th century. It's thought to come from a particular fighting style in which the swordsman held a short sword in one hand, and a buckler (a small shield) in the other. The buckler not only provided some protection against attack, but was also used as a weapon — basically for bashing enemies on the head! The term swashbuckler started to be used in books and films to describe any brave and talented swordsman.

> # Rachel Wall was America's first female pirate

As we've read, piracy wasn't just a job for the boys, but was Rachel Wall a groundbreaker — the first American woman to pursue the profession of piracy?

⭐ And the truth is...

You bet she was! Born Rachel Schmidt, on a small farm in Pennsylvania, the young woman met a fisherman called George Wall down by the docks one day, and the pair became loved-up outlaws of the high seas. The Walls' trick was to position Rachel on deck after a storm, calling for help. When passersby pulled alongside, they were killed and all their valuables stolen! The Walls and their crew captured 12 boats in all, stealing $6,000 in cash, loads of valuables, and killing 24 sailors between 1781–82. Not surprisingly, Rachel and her hubby were eventually caught and hanged. Pirate fact: Rachel Wall was the last woman hanged in Massachusetts.

Verdict:

WHERE DID MOST PIRATES COME FROM?

Pirates were a mixed bunch of fortune hunters from all over the world. Here's where they called home:

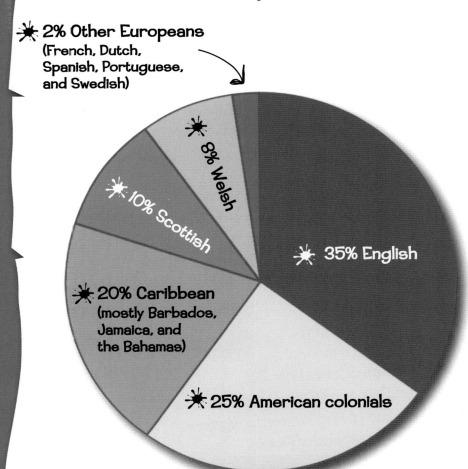

2% Other Europeans (French, Dutch, Spanish, Portuguese, and Swedish)

8% Welsh

10% Scottish

20% Caribbean (mostly Barbados, Jamaica, and the Bahamas)

35% English

25% American colonials

FAMOUS PIRATE TRIALS

What happened to the most famous pirates? Were they hanged, imprisoned or reprieved?

November 1720
Spanish Town, Jamaica
Calico Jack Rackham and his crew
10 executed, including Rackham

HANGED

November 1720
Spanish Town, Jamaica
Mary Read and Anne Bonny
Found guilty but not hanged, as they were both pregnant

IMPRISONED

March 1719, Williamsburg
15 of Blackbeard's men
13 were hanged. Israel Hands, Blackbeard's second-in-command, was reprieved for giving evidence against corrupt government officials

HANGED AND REPRIEVED

October 1718, Charleston
Major Stede Bonnet
30 hanged, including Bonnet

HANGED

March 1722, Cape Coast
Castle, West Africa
Bartholomew Roberts' crew
52 hanged, 74 acquitted,
37 imprisoned

HANGED, REPRIEVED, & IMPRISONED

March 1721,
Spanish Town, Jamaica
Captain Charles Vane
Hanged at Gallows Point
(now a popular holiday resort!)

HANGED

October 1722,
Nassau, Bahamas
Captain Blanco's crew
5 men executed

HANGED

July 1723, London
Captain Philip Roche
Hanged at Execution Dock

HANGED

March 1724, St. Kitts,
West Indies
Captain Lowther's crew
11 men hanged

HANGED

March 1725, London
Captain Gow and his crew
10 hanged at Execution Dock,
including Gow

HANGED

Blackbeard's headless body swam around his ship

Few pirates died of old age, and Blackbeard was no exception. He eventually met his end in November 1718 when he boarded a British Royal Navy ship in Bath Harbor, North Carolina, with a small crew, and was outnumbered. Blackbeard was about to kill the ship's captain when one of the British crew slashed Blackbeard's neck with his cutlass. The pirate kept fighting, but eventually died from blood loss.

⭐ And the truth is...

Blackbeard was a tough cookie who needed shooting five times and stabbing 20 times — and having his head nearly chopped off — before he finally breathed his last. The victorious captain, Lieutenant Maynard, proudly displayed Blackbeard's head on the bow of his ship. The body he threw over the side where, legend has it, it swam alongside the ship for several miles before disappearing. Don't know about you, but we suspect that's *not* true!

Verdict: **PHONY**

The Archbishop of York was a pirate

Pirates and priests might both start with a "p" but we imagine that's where the similarities end. So was the Archbishop of York really a former swashbuckling pirate? Read on to find out.

⭐ And the truth is...

According to a number of sources, Oxford-University-educated Lancelot Blackburne was a penniless priest in the Caribbean who decided to supplement his income by becoming a buccaneer. When he eventually put his pirating days behind him, he returned to the cloth in England. Was he hanged for piracy? No, he was made Archbishop of York. Who says crime doesn't pay? Pirate fact: Blackburne liked to bend the rules even when he was Archbishop. So the story goes, he secretly married George I and his mistress, and was rumored to employ famous robber Dick Turpin as his butler!

Verdict:  (hopefully) FACT

English pirate Henry Morgan was knighted by the Queen

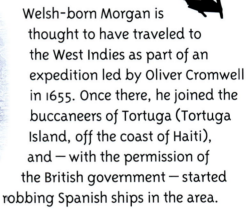

Welsh-born Morgan is thought to have traveled to the West Indies as part of an expedition led by Oliver Cromwell in 1655. Once there, he joined the buccaneers of Tortuga (Tortuga Island, off the coast of Haiti), and — with the permission of the British government — started robbing Spanish ships in the area. When suitable ships became scarce, he began to attack Spanish settlements, including the famous capture of Panama City in 1671. (During the siege, his men were so short of food they had to eat leather bags, cut into strips, and softened in boiling water!)

★ And the truth is...

The British and Spanish governments eventually made friends and Morgan feared he would be hanged as a pirate. However, the British authorities waited for protests to die down, and knighted Morgan as a thank-you for his efforts.

FACT

Verdict:

GLOSSARY

arsenal a place where weapons are stored

authorities people in charge

brimstone sulfur (a nonmetallic element used in many industries)

captive one who is held prisoner

crucify to put to death by nailing or binding the wrists or hands and feet to a cross

cutlass a short curving sword formerly used by sailors on warships

enlisted members of the military who rank below commissioned or warrant officers

far-flung widely spread or distributed

galleon a heavy sailing ship with square sails used by Spain from the 15th to 18th centuries

gibbet an iron cage used to hold prisoners

looting to rob, especially on a large scale and usually by violence

malicious having or showing a desire to cause harm to someone

marooned to leave a person alone on a deserted island

mercenary a soldier hired to fight for another country

merchant ship a ship used in commerce

mutineer one who takes part in a mutiny

mutiny revolt (as of a naval crew) against discipline or a superior officer

piracy an act of robbery on the high seas

plunder to take goods by force

raider pirate

reprieve to delay punishment

seafarer a person who navigates or assists in navigating a ship

supplement to add or supply additions

swashbuckler sword fighter

uninhabited not occupied by people

FOR MORE INFORMATION

BOOKS

Arias, Oscar and Children's History Press. *101 Amazing Pirate Facts.* Sarasota, FL: Children's History Press, 2014.

Doty, Eldon, Sarah Knott, and Sean Stewart Price. *Pirates: Truth and Rumors.* New York: Capstone, 2010.

Hamilton, John. *Pirate Ships & Weapons.* Edina MN: ABDO, 2010.

WEBSITES

5 Pirate Myths . . . And the Facts that Belie Them
http://blog.press.princeton.edu/2009/04/23/5-pirate-myths-and-the-facts-that-belie-them/

9 Pirate Myths Exposed for Talk-Like-a-Pirate Day
http://geekdad.com/2014/09/9-pirate-myths-exposed/

Parrots, Peg-legs, Plunder — Debunking Pirate Myths
http://www.todayifoundout.com/index.php/2014/08/parrots-peg-legs-plunder-debunking-pirate-myths/

Where can I find myths about...